THE PROFFITTS OF RIDGEWOOD

When the Ridgewood started serving wood-cooked ham, thinly sliced, with a Kansas City-style sauce, no one would have guessed that this family restaurant in rural East Tennessee would become a pilgrimage site for barbecue lovers, many of whom believe that its unique barbecue is the best in the world. Fred Sauceman, our foremost chronicler of Appalachian foodways, tells us how this happened, and it is a fascinating story, well told.

JOHN SHELTON REED

co-author of *Holy Smoke: The Big Book of North Carolina Barbecue*
and "Eminence Grease" of the Campaign for Real Barbecue at TrueCue.org

Fred Sauceman is more qualified than anyone else I know to enter the "dangerous territory" of today's American barbecue scene and tell it like he sees it, which turns out to be how it is. If somebody raved about a joint where ham is the specialty and the blue cheese dressing is a standout dip by itself, sans salad, I'd have scruples about their credibility. Not so when that somebody is Fred. His gifted ability to put you in the scene—the hills, hollers, flora, aromas, and most of all the people of East Tennessee—is second only to his mouth-watering details of the feast that awaits you when you're lucky enough to be seated at the Ridgewood. Take home a jar of Grace Proffitt's sauce. You will crave more later!

ARDIE A. DAVIS

founder of the American Royal International Barbecue Sauce Contest
author and co-author of eleven barbecue books
and Barbecue Hall of Fame inductee

Barbecue, perhaps more than any other American food, still speaks of place. Yes, Fred Sauceman knows barbecue. Take a trip to the epicenter of Appalachian foodways with a man who was born, raised, and, more importantly, has eaten his way through this region. Salivate as he describes Ridgewood Barbecue's smoked fresh hams emerging from the real hickory wood-fired pits. Fred's words take your mind on an Appalachian expedition. The mounds of thinly carved smoked pork goodness beckon you to make the journey in person to Bluff City, Tennessee.

CHRIS LILLY

Pitmaster & Partner, Big Bob Gibson Bar-B-Q
author of *Big Bob Gibson's BBQ Book* and *Fire & Smoke*
and Barbecue Hall of Fame inductee

FOOD *and the* AMERICAN *South*

This series explores the central and profound role that food and foodways play in understanding the South's past, its present, and its future. Through a broad variety of academic disciplines, the series examines the region's culinary history, celebrates the glories of the Southern table, and analyzes the many influences that come together to define Southern food.

—Fred W. Sauceman, Series Editor

In the series

The Proffitts of Ridgewood: An Appalachian Family's Life in Barbecue
Fred W. Sauceman

Cook & Tell: Recipes and Stories from Southern Kitchens
Johnathon Scott Barrett, ed.

MERCER UNIVERSITY

MERCER UNIVERSITY PRESS

Endowed by

TOM WATSON BROWN

and

THE WATSON-BROWN FOUNDATION, INC.

The PROFFITTS of Ridgewood

AN APPALACHIAN FAMILY'S LIFE IN BARBECUE

FRED W. SAUCEMAN

MERCER UNIVERSITY PRESS | MACON, GEORGIA | 2017

MUP/ P550

978-0-88146-627-0

Published by Mercer University Press
1501 Mercer University Drive
Macon, Georgia 31207

FIRST EDITION

9 8 7 6 5 4 3 2 1

Books published by Mercer University Press are printed on acid-free paper
that meets the requirements of the American National Standard for Information Sciences—
Permanence of Paper for Printed Library Materials.

Book design by Burt&Burt
Printed in Canada

Cataloging-in-Publication Data is available from the Library of Congress

To the Proffitt family,
who stayed with hog.

Preface: Entering Dangerous Territory **11**

Why Ridgewood? **17**

An Appalachian Story **21**

Entering Bullock's Hollow **25**

Jim and Grace **27**

Beginnings **31**

The Long Arm of the Government **37**

Building and Tending the Pit **39**

High on the Hog **43**

A Family Heirloom and Rite of Passage: The Sauce **45**

A Prescription for Great Beans **55**

Blue Cheese Bounty **63**

Placing the Order: A Tale of Two Slaws **65**

Ridgewood and Racing **71**

Grace on the Job **77**

The Ridgewood Rundown **85**

Getting There **87**

An American Story **89**

Acknowledgments **91**

Preface

Entering Dangerous Territory

Writing a book about barbecue is in many ways a dangerous endeavor. Barbecue's ability to spark fights is legendary. As emotional as people in my world are about chicken and dumplings—whether they should be rolled and flat or dropped and fluffy—the intensity of the dumpling debate cannot come close to barbecue's feather-ruffling potential.

Barbecue fuels fights for a lot of reasons. Foremost among them is the infinite number of variables and questions to be filled in and answered when it comes time to cook. What animal should I choose? What part of that animal? What type of cooker is best? What is the proper fuel or heat source? Should I rub? Should I baste? If I sauce at all, what type of sauce should I use? Once the meat is done, there arises the oft-debated and very basic question of exactly what to do with it. Should it be pulled? Should it be sliced? Should it be chopped? Should it be minced?

There is only one Ridgewood Barbecue. Photo by Larry Smith.

Decisions about side dishes and desserts further complicate the equation. Should my slaw be white or red or yellow? Each of these stages of the barbecue process brings forth opinions, and strong ones.

Despite this minefield of attitudes and approaches, I'm glad people still fight, at least verbally, over barbecue. The answers to the questions I've posed here are largely dictated by region. Yes, I can find yellow sauce from South Carolina in East Tennessee now and Alabama white sauce in the Chelsea Market in Manhattan, but barbecue, perhaps more than any other American food, still speaks of place. Asserting the supposed superiority of one sauce over another or one rack of ribs over another is driven not just by taste but also by regional pride. In an increasingly homogenized America, barbecue, like dialects and accents, is still understood and appreciated in the context of geography.

As my good friend Dr. John Shelton Reed, an East Tennessean and University of North Carolina Professor Emeritus, is fond of saying, barbecue in the South is indeed like the wines and cheeses of Europe.

Drive 100 miles and the barbecue does change, at least in the locally owned places. Shelby, North Carolina, is exactly two hours and fifteen minutes from my Johnson City, Tennessee, doorstep. In Shelby, at Bridges Barbecue Lodge, a perennially matriarchal business now run by a former beauty queen, I encounter a side dish not to be found in East Tennessee barbecue joints: hushpuppies. And I find coleslaw totally devoid of mayonnaise.

I also find, at Bridges, a woodpile, perhaps the quickest tip-off of all that good barbecue awaits. I've noted on several visits the mathematical precision of that pile. The logs are so even and linear that they seem to have been arranged by someone using a straight edge. Although the styles of barbecue differ, Bridges shares a kinship with Ridgewood, the subject of this book. The two restaurants are close to the same age, and for most of their history, women have called the shots, which may well be the reason for that orderly woodpile. Finally, in the messy business of barbecue, the two restaurants are spotlessly clean.

A full parking lot is a typical scene at The Ridgewood. Photo by Charlie Warden.

My appreciation of barbecue is ecumenical. Although I'm a lifelong resident of East Tennessee, I embrace the vinegar-and-pepper sauces of Eastern North Carolina and crave the dips of the Piedmont. I savor the mustardy, German-inspired sauces stretching from Charleston through Columbia, South Carolina. I advocate for the white sauce of Decatur, Alabama, created in 1925 by former railroad man Big Bob Gibson, who baptized barbecued chickens with his peppery creation. I even eat that white sauce on fried potatoes and onions. I love Memphis pork shoulder, and I can take my ribs wet or dry. I respect the mutton barbecue of Owensboro, Kentucky, on equal par with the smoked shoulder clods of Lockhart, Texas.

Fall Color
Without the Crowds
RIDGEWOOD MENU
Grilled
Western T-Bone Steak
One Pound and One-Quarter of the finest juicy Western T-Bone Steak. Grilled the way you like it. Served with Golden Brown French Fried Potatoes, Salad, Hot Bake and Serve Rolls, Butter, Jelly and Coffee.
$2.95
Sirloin Steak
One Pound and One-Quarter of the Best Western Sirloin Steak cooked on the grill any way you like it. Served with Golden Brown French Fried Potatoes, Salad, Hot Bake and Serve Rolls, Butter, Jelly, and Coffee.
$2.95
Country Ham Steak
One Center Cut of Country Ham aged and cured until it reaches the peak of good taste. Skillet fried in its own natural juices. Served with French Fries, Salad, Hot Biscuits, Brown Gravy, Butter, Honey and Coffee.
$2.95
Country Style Fried Chicken
One-Half of a tender young Fryer fried to a golden brown country style. Served with Chicken Gravy, French Fries, Salad, Hot Biscuits, Butter, Honey, and Coffee.
$1.85
Chicken in a Box
One-Half of a tender young Fryer, fried to a golden brown country style, served with Shoe String Potatoes, Hot Buttered Bake and Serve Rolls and Honey.
$1.45
SPECIAL ORDERS
Small T-Bone Steak $1.65
Small Sirloin Steak $1.65
Sugar Cured Ham Steak $1.45
Bar-B-Q Pork Dinner $1.25
Cubed Steak 95c
Hamburger Steak 95c
Veal Cutlets
Pork Chops
Oysters (half fry) (in season)
Shrimp (French Fried)
Fish (Red Perch)
COCKTAILS
Oyster Cocktail (in season)
Shrimp Cocktail
SALADS
Special Combination Salad
Head Lettuce Salad with our home made Roquefort dressing
Sandwich
Hot Dog
Hamburger
Cheeseburger
Bacon and Tomato
Bacon and Egg
Grilled Cheese
Baked Ham
Any Sandwich
Oyster
French
Chili
Country Ham and
Sugar Cured Ham
Bacon and Eggs
Sausage and Eggs
Pie
Coffee
Sweet Milk
Butter Milk
Juices

Ridgewood Restaurant
Menu
HIGHWAY 19-E
Route #?
BLUFF CITY, TENNESSEE
PHONE 538-5532
Breakfasts
FAMILY WEEKEND GETAWAYS UNDER $500
Exclusive Interview!
FANNIE FLAGG ON HER NEW BOOK

Why Ridgewood?

**"This is not just some electric device.
This is a real barbecue pit."**
Larry Proffitt

While maintaining that spirit of barbecue inclusiveness, when asked to name my favorite, I answer instantly and confidently: Ridgewood Barbecue in Bluff City, Tennessee. I won't make the mistake of saying it's the best barbecue in America, as a couple of writers once did. To say that would assume I've tasted all the barbecue in America, an ambitious but impossible assignment. Yes, Ridgewood is my favorite. And flavor is only one of the many reasons.

When it comes to pork, I don't know of anyone in America more knowledgeable than my good friend Allan Benton, owner of Benton's Smoky Mountain Country Hams in Madisonville, Tennessee. His ham and bacon are heralded nationwide.

"I had been told that Ridgewood was the best barbecue in East Tennessee," Allan tells me. "Still, I was not expecting too much. After all, I have driven many miles out of my way just chasing a rumor of good barbecue, only to come away thinking it was good but not worth the drive. I had been told that Ridgewood uses hams instead of butts or shoulders. The plate arrived with the thinly sliced ham piled high on the bun. It took only one bite to know that Ridgewood lives up to the

Grace Proffitt, at right, in a photograph that was used on the Ridgewood menu for years. We posed her son Larry and granddaughter Lisa in the same spot and brought the family back together through digital technology. Composite photo by Larry Smith.

accolades and incredible reputation. Ridgewood shares equal billing for great barbecue with its Memphis 'cousins' and is among the best barbecue joints anywhere in the South."

Early in the fall semester at East Tennessee State University, in my course, "The Foodways of Appalachia," I outline for my students the qualities and characteristics that I think make a good food story. Ridgewood meets pretty much all of those criteria. Among the hundreds of restaurants my wife Jill and I have covered for various assignments over the years, Ridgewood stands out, in our opinion, as the one place in the East Tennessee region that is truly worthy of book-length treatment.

Among those criteria for a good food story, longevity and continuity are at the top. Since it first opened its doors in 1948, Ridgewood has never moved from its place in beautiful Bullock's Hollow. The menu may have changed—as we'll see, barbecue was not among the restaurant's original offerings—but the location and ownership have remained constant.

Ownership by the same family is another measure in my classroom scale. Ridgewood qualifies again. It has always been owned by the Proffitt family—first Grace and Jim, then their sons Terry and Larry, and now Larry's daughter Lisa. When Lisa's children are old enough to take over the business, assuming hopes and plans work out, the restaurant will be in its fourth generation of family ownership. This is a story of smoked meat, but in a larger sense, it's the story of an Appalachian family.

When people ask me what makes a good restaurant, I don't start with the food. I start with the presence of the owners. When I stop for a bowl of Beans All the Way at The Bean Barn in Greeneville, Tennessee, I want to see Jerry and Donna Hartsell behind the counter. When I visit The Dip Dog Stand in Smyth County, Virginia, I want to see a Hall—Grant or Pam or one of their children, maybe even Crystal with her doctorate in education—spearing my red hot dog, dousing it in an Appalachian tempura, and painting it with mustard. When I'm ready for Thai curry in the mountains of East Tennessee, I want to make sure Prayoon and Rachel Royston are in their kitchen at Monsoon in Butler to serve it. At Ridgewood, I expect to see a Proffitt. I want to know that the hands of Lisa Proffitt Peters crafted my blue cheese dressing and stirred my barbecue sauce. I want to know that her dad, Larry, proclaimed it "Good enough to sell." The presence of the owners separates the places I love and respect from the anonymous, absentee-owned chains, whose dollars enhance corporate coffers outside the region.

Gas and electricity are not used in cooking barbecue at The Ridgewood. The woodpile on the hill behind the restaurant tells the story. Photo by Fred Sauceman.

Of course, choosing a topic for a food story gets almost nowhere without a quality product to describe. Ridgewood barbecues fresh ham, and the pitmasters there do it exceedingly well. Ham, high on the hog, is the only cut of pork barbecue you can order. Both the pork and the beef are produced without the use of compromising shortcuts. There is no gas in the process. There is no electricity. Those hams and beef are fueled and flavored by hickory wood, fire, and smoke, which leads to another criterion for a good food story: adherence to tradition.

Hardly a week passes without a visit from a salesperson trying to convince Larry and Lisa to give up the laborious process of smoking hams and beef over hickory wood. "We can sell you an electric cooker or a gas cooker," those salespeople will say, "and you can just press a button, go home, and forget about it." That pressure to convert to gas-powered or electric cookers occurs with relentless regularity. But the Proffitts resist the temptation. They send those salespeople on down the road. The Proffitts realize that the most important ingredient in the cookery of Appalachia is the investment of time. It makes all the difference.

These are the reasons I have chosen to tell the Ridgewood story.

An Appalachian Story

"I like people who haven't forgotten their roots."
Larry Proffitt

In the Proffitt family, I find many of the noble values that define the Southern Appalachian region. It's a region where I was born, where I was educated, and where I have always worked. I will never leave it. My affection for the people of Appalachia began with my parents. My father, along with his parents and eleven brothers and sisters, sharecropped in the Orebank and Bright Hope communities of Greene County, Tennessee. My mother was the child of public servants who lived in town and navigated through the Great Depression with little financial suffering. My maternal grandfather patrolled the streets of Greeneville, Tennessee, as Night Chief of Police. My maternal grandmother staffed the town's telephone switchboard. My father made televisions, and my mother made dresses. My family understood the nobility of hard work. My people understood the importance of frugality in any kind of economy. In

Ridgewood Barbecue has been at the same location and in the same family since 1948. Photo by Fred Sauceman.

flush times they saved. In hard times they saved. They persisted on, never giving up, no matter what hardships temporarily blocked their path. Most of all, they loved their part of the world and never wished to leave it.

I find the same qualities in the Proffitt family. When Larry Proffitt headed off to pharmacy school at the University of Tennessee in Memphis, he knew he would return to the hills and hollows of his home place, and he has never left. The education he received on the banks of the Mississippi River in the 1960s improved his lot in life, but folks who have known him a long time are quick to say that education never changed him. Nor did it alter his beautiful Appalachian mountain accent, still clear today in the cadence of his voice, the hardness of his vowels. As so many people in these mountains are, Larry is a born storyteller. His stories and his philosophies are the foundation of this book. His education is deep, but his wisdom is natural. As I tell my students each fall, he is one of the smartest and wisest people I know.

The Proffitts have never lived an extravagant lifestyle. As Larry often says, "We were just poor folks, trying to make a living." For much of his life, he has worked two jobs, as a restaurant owner and manager in Bluff City and as a pharmacist in Elizabethton. He had good role models. His father Jim made rayon in Elizabethton and barbecue sauce in Bluff City. His mother walked the creaking floors of country stores stocking shelves and then embraced the morning-until-night life of a restaurant owner.

It would have been easy, at The Ridgewood, to give in to less laborious cooking methods. But the Proffitts never have. In barbecue, just as in life, they have learned that the easy way is rarely the best way.

Over the years, when government policies forced them to retool their business, when highways passed them by, when death decimated their ranks, when dietary fears gripped America, the Proffitts never thought of giving up. It simply wasn't in their DNA. When they faced hardships, they kept on without complaint. Tough times only helped them appreciate what they had all the more.

When lawyers and businesspeople talk franchising or outright purchase, as they do often today, the Proffitts send them packing, too. The Ridgewood, Larry tells them, is not for sale. "It won't be for sale. We're going to do the same thing we've been doing all these years. No change."

Love of the land, respect for tradition, veneration of hard work, defiance of adversity, and admiringly stubborn independence. These characteristics aren't unique to Appalachia, but in combination, they are characteristics that strongly define Appalachia. They are the values that have made Ridgewood an Appalachian and an American institution.

Bullock's Hollow, Sullivan County, Tennessee. Photo by Larry Smith.

Entering Bullock's Hollow

"They're in here from all walks of life. Some of them have trouble rubbing two nickels together, while others have the kind of American Express card that you have to have a million dollars to get. And you have everybody in between there. You're all the same when you come in. We have them come in here from all over the world. A restaurant with an hour wait out in the middle of nowhere—they're not used to seeing that. Saturday night is our busiest. People will be waiting since 3:30 and we don't open until 4:30. When we open the door, we'll have a full house within three or four minutes."

Ray Harrington, manager, Ridgewood Barbecue

The Old Elizabethton Highway winds through and bisects Bullock's Hollow, revealing beauty around every gentle curve. In some places, the hillsides that hug the highway are almost straight up. The hollow fits the classic definition of the word perfectly. In East Tennessee, we often call them "hollers." It's a dialectal variation, but somehow the sound makes sense. Carter and Sullivan counties are full of them, many named for the families who have occupied the land for generations.

In the flat spaces cradled by those hills, families take advantage of precious sunlight by growing magnificent gardens. Rows of half-runner and Kentucky Wonder green beans, and others bearing the names of families who have nurtured them longer than anyone can remember, grow alongside yellow and white corn and yellow summer squash. Those hill-hugged gardens differ very little from the ones Native Americans planted long before white settlement of the area. Along the gentler sloping hillsides, wild turkeys forage for food and occasionally saunter across the road.

Cross Indian Creek a couple of times and you're nearing Ridgewood Barbecue. It may have a Bluff City address, but there's no evidence of a town in sight. You're in the country, in the hills. Round a curve in Sullivan County and there it is, set tightly against a wooded hillside. On a good day, when the wind is right, hickory smoke gives you a half-mile signal that barbecue is near. Drive a little closer and you hear the crunch of wheels meeting gravel. Vehicles of all descriptions, with license plates from all over America, converge here, no matter the time of day.

As Grace Proffitt once said, "If you have good food, folks'll find you."

Jim and Grace

"We were just poor folks, trying to make a living."
Larry Proffitt

Ridgewood patriarch Jim Proffitt grew up on a farm in the Rock Hill community, on the Sullivan-Carter County line, about three miles from where The Ridgewood now stands. That Tennessee farm, now consisting of 186 acres, has been in the same family since 1856. Larry Proffitt possesses the original deeds, from the time when the land was sold to his paternal great-grandmother, Sarah Masengill Peregoy, and her husband Dabner, who was of French extraction. The Proffitt side of the family came across the mountain to East Tennessee from Banner Elk, in Avery County, North Carolina, in a covered wagon. Stories of Native Americans coming out of the hollows to ask for food have been passed down through the Proffitt family, just like those old deeds.

"Just across the gravel road, my grandpa, Taylor Wade Proffitt, had a little store," says Larry Proffitt. "And I was told years ago that he would lend people things, but he would write their names down, make a note of when the item was borrowed and when the borrower promised to bring it back. Because a lot of people would come and borrow stuff, and you'd never see it again. He had a little store, and my daddy converted that into a house for us."

That house still stands today, serving as a depository for records from Elizabethton's Burgie Drug Store, owned by the Proffitt family. The house originally included three rooms and was warmed by a coal heater in the front room. The house was humble and unassuming, but it kept the family together.

Jim Proffitt, Larry's father, began working at the American Bemberg plant in Elizabethton in 1928, three years after it was founded. He was laid off after about a year on the job. Once production started booming again, he resumed his former position in the spinning department. He made synthetic silk, known as rayon, and he worked at Bemberg for the rest of his professional life. During World War II, the plant manufactured cloth for parachutes.

Jim was offered supervisory positions on several occasions at Bemberg, but he would never take them. He would settle for less pay in order to be covered by the union. Jim's job was that important to the family's survival. His years in the factory, around high-pitched machines, eventually took their toll, and he lost most of his hearing. Larry recalls that his mother-in-law, who died at age ninety-eight, worked in a shirt factory in LaFollette, Tennessee, and suffered the same kind of hearing loss.

Jim worked alternating shifts at Bemberg—days one week, three o'clock until eleven o'clock at night the next week, and then graveyard the next, before starting the grueling cycle over again. "It was tough duty," says Larry. "It was physical work. He always told Terry and me to get an education so we could work with our brains instead of our backs like he did. He only got to go through the eighth grade."

Larry remembers his father as gregarious and outgoing. "And he loved to farm," says Larry. "He had raised cattle since he was a teenager. He loved to ride a tractor. After we started serving barbecue, he might come in until eleven o'clock or twelve and make sauce, and then he'd say, 'See you, Mama,' and head to the farm."

Ridgewood matriarch Grace, whose maiden name was Reynolds, was born in Easley, South Carolina. After her high school gradua-

Opposite page: "I had two little boys to raise," said the persistent Grace Proffitt, pictured here with her husband Jim and sons Terry and Larry. Photo courtesy Larry Proffitt.

Larry Proffitt at the old home place, on land that has been in the family since 1856. Photo by Fred Sauceman.

tion, the family moved to Northeast Tennessee and took up residence near the rock quarry in the historic community of Watauga. Her father was superintendent of the quarry, the same kind of work he had done back in Upstate South Carolina.

In their earlier years, both Grace and Jim worked in country stores. East Tennessee was full of them at the time. Almost every community had one in an era before the coming of large supermarkets. In those wood-floored, un-air-conditioned country stores, Grace first learned to deal with the public. She learned patience. She developed confidence in her abilities. She learned the value of a dollar. Grace ran a store on Highland Hill near Elizabethton and then another about a mile and a half from the spot where The Ridgewood would be built. She sold such items as Nehi soft drinks, potted meat, Vienna sausages, potato chips, fried pies, bubble gum, and MoonPies. As she worked, she tended to the needs of her two sons, Larry in toddlerhood and Terry in babyhood.

Beginnings

"I work every day. I get here before nine o'clock and stay until the lights are turned off of the night."

The late Grace Proffitt

In 1948, Grace and Jim decided to take the experience and knowledge they had gained in running country stores and apply them to their first and, as it would turn out, only restaurant venture.

First they had to figure out what to call the new business. When most diners nowadays ponder the origin of the Ridgewood name, they assume an East Tennessee mountain connection. The name fits the

The Ridgewood Hotel and Grill, Daytona Beach, Florida, where Grace and Jim Proffitt came up with the name for their restaurant. Postcard in the author's possession.

One of the earliest known photographs of Grace Proffitt in her Bluff City, Tennessee, restaurant. Photo courtesy Larry Proffitt.

restaurant perfectly. East Tennessee is a region of alternating ridges and valleys, and the restaurant sits in a heavily wooded area. Oddly, though, Grace and Jim Proffitt got the idea for the name a long way from the ridges and the woods of East Tennessee.

Their favorite vacation spot was Daytona Beach, Florida, even though they often had to borrow money from the credit union at Beaunit Fibers in Elizabethton to get there. While at Daytona Beach on a trip with their two boys, Grace and Jim noticed The Ridgewood Hotel and Grill. It had once been a private home. Travel literature of the day described the hotel as "one of Daytona's most fashionable places to spend the winter." Located on U.S. Highway 1, The Ridgewood was known for its tropical gardens. And the city was bisected by a Ridgewood Avenue.

Grace and Jim liked the sound of Ridgewood as a restaurant name and never gave it a second thought. Later, we'll see that Daytona Beach was the origin of a second idea, one that would radically change the future of what was, at first, Ridgewood Grill.

As he was beginning the business, Jim enlisted two partners, Paul Bare and Homer Davis. Four years after the restaurant opened, Bare sold his interest to Jim. Davis owned the other third until Jim bought him out years later. Bare left East Tennessee, as part of what would be called the "Appalachian Diaspora," seeking work and better pay up north. He landed a job with Ford Motor Company in Detroit and eventually retired from there.

For Grace, opening a restaurant in a lonely, fairly secluded mountain hollow was a risky endeavor. Jim would continue his work at the rayon plant and fill in at the restaurant when he could. Oftentimes, his plucky wife was left to oversee things, but she never felt threatened or unsafe, even when she came to work one morning and found a bullet hole in the stainless steel section of the wall that is now behind the grill.

The Proffitts still laugh about that bullet hole. As Larry recalls, "Paul Bare was working as a night watchman. He'd sleep in here, on a cot. One night he was walking through here, and he had his gun, and he let it go off accidentally, shooting a hole in that stainless steel. And it's been here that long. He was only here four years, so it had to be 1949 or 1950. That's a nine-millimeter hole."

Larry points to the bullet hole in the stainless steel. Photo by Fred Sauceman.

Jim cut all the hickory wood off the Proffitt farm to build the restaurant, and those joists, beams, and rafters support the structure to this day. He hauled the wood from the farm to the building site in a large log truck. Larry remembers seeing the original outline of the restaurant, marked by string wrapped around sticks. In 1980, the year of Jim's death, the Proffitts

An early menu from The Ridgewood Grill. Photo by Fred Sauceman.

modified the architecture by building around the original structure.

While the name Ridgewood is now synonymous with barbecue throughout East Tennessee and far beyond, it did not start out that way. The business began as a beer joint, a roadhouse.

"Used to be, there were beer joints everywhere up and down the road," recalls Larry. "They would serve hamburgers and country ham and such."

An early menu from The Ridgewood Grill featured grilled western T-bone steak that weighed in at a pound and a quarter, "grilled the way you like it." Golden brown French-fried potatoes, salad, hot "bake and serve" rolls, butter, jelly, and coffee rounded out the repast.

For the same price, $2.95, diners could select a center-cut country ham steak, "cured until it reaches the peak of good taste. Skillet fried in its own natural juices." French fries, salad, hot biscuits, and brown gravy completed the plate.

The Ridgewood built an early reputation on country-style fried chicken, a menu item that would eventually be abandoned because of the long wait time it involved. Grace served half of a young fryer, chicken gravy, and biscuits.

"Everything was put in little white paper bags," says Larry. "There weren't any plastic bags back then. And they would freeze the chicken. If somebody came in here and ordered chicken, this was an hour and a half deal. They'd have to take that chicken out of the freezer. They'd put it in hot water and then pull the bag off of it. It had to sit there until it thawed.

"And then they'd bread it and they'd fry it in shortening. Right here on the stove. They'd fry it just like you'd fry it at home. You can imagine the time. It was so labor-intensive, but people wanted it."

Grace's chicken was always bone-in. And her source, for both chicken and country ham, was Donald Davidson's Grocery on Elk Avenue in Elizabethton.

At the bottom of that early menu is a section called "Cocktails." There is a shrimp cocktail and an oyster cocktail (in season), both priced at 75 cents. The shrimp version was fairly commonplace at the time, even in land-locked Tennessee, but the oysters, served this way, must have been a rarity.

"What I remember from a little boy is the coming of the fish truck," Larry tells me. "It had 'Chesapeake Bay' on the side, and it would park out front. It was about the size of a pickup truck, but it had a refrigerator container on the back of it. And Mama would buy oysters, and they came in a gallon can. It looked like a gallon latex paint can of today. It had blue and white writing on the outside.

"One day my wife Norma and I were on the antique trail in New York, and I said, 'There's one of those cans, an oyster can.'"

Larry says the fact that his mother served an oyster cocktail in those days, with oysters that were likely raw, still fascinates him.

In the wintertime, Grace would make oyster stew for farmers as they sat on the restaurant's counter stools, waiting to be fed on their break from the fields. Grace's oyster stew recipe does not survive, but Larry remembers the main ingredients being whole milk, butter, salt, pepper, and oysters off that memorable truck from the Maryland shores. "She had to stir it constantly to prevent it from scalding," he adds.

In the "Special Orders" section of that menu were fried oysters and shrimp, and the fish Grace fried was red perch. The shrimp and oysters were dipped in egg and rolled in cracker meal. "We sold a lot of fried oysters," says Larry.

Ridgewood diners once pressed buzzers for service. Photo by Larry Smith.

There was a time, too, when Ridgewood served breakfast. Country ham and eggs were on the menu back then. Morning drink options were "Sweet Milk" (a term common in Appalachia to differentiate regular milk from buttermilk), "Butter Milk" (listed just that way, as two words), and thirty-five-cent milkshakes.

Ordering was different back then. Walk into the back dining room of the restaurant today and you'll see buttons on the wall. They were disconnected long ago, but they remain as a reminder of how servers were once summoned to the tables with buzzers.

The Long Arm of the Government

"Stay with the pig until he makes a hog."
Grace Proffitt

Appalachian people are well known for their resistance to governmental interference. That trait, of course, is most obvious in the region's moonshine culture and attempts to escape "revenuers." A governmental decision in 1952 would have a profound effect on the future of The Ridgewood Grill. That year, Sullivan County, Tennessee, went dry. Grace and Jim had depended on beer sales for a good portion of their revenue at the grill. Suddenly, though, that source literally dried up. It's the reason Paul Bare decided to bail out after only four years as a business partner with Jim Proffitt.

But Grace and Jim, true to their mountain upbringing, refused to give up. They would never leave their beloved hollow. Larry especially credits his mother for keeping the doors open, for "staying with it no matter what." In her memorable words, "Stay with the pig until he makes a hog."

An early sign, once the restaurant had converted to barbecue. Photo courtesy Larry Proffitt.

Alcohol hasn't been served at The Ridgewood since 1952. Sweet tea is the beverage of choice. As writer Rick Bragg of Alabama once said when we were eating at The Ridgewood, "Unsweet tea is brown water." Servers like Kimberly Guess understand the perfect pairing between barbecue and sweet tea. Photo by Larry Smith.

Years later, Grace recalled that period in her life: "I had to do something. I had two little boys to raise."

Jim and Grace were worried about the future, but they didn't let those two little boys know it. They borrowed money again and took a family vacation trip back to their favorite spot, Daytona Beach, Florida. There, they made a life-changing business decision that would ultimately redefine their restaurant. And they made it largely by accident.

"In Daytona Beach, we went out walking, and we saw people smoking chickens," Larry remembers. "My father was always looking for a new way to cook something that would be unique. And so we went out and they were barbecuing chickens. They had the fire over here, and they were piping smoke over to where the meat was, through indirect heat. That's what gave my parents the idea to transform that former roadhouse, that former beer joint, into a barbecue restaurant."

Rather than chicken, though, the Proffitts chose to start cooking pork, since it is largely the meat of choice for barbecue in East Tennessee. Eventually beef—barbecued top round—would be added to the menu. Server Dianna Blumenstock, who has worked at The Ridgewood since 2003, says that on occasion customers will ask the difference between pork and beef, and that always elicits a laugh. "We hear all kinds of comments," she says. "When I first started at The Ridgewood, the bathrooms were outside. When someone would ask where the bathrooms were, we would tell them outside. Their eyes would get as big as half dollars, thinking they would be going to an outhouse."

Building and Tending the Pit

"If you don't see smoke, you're not eating barbecue. If you see gas or electricity, you're not eating barbecue."

Mike Blevins, owner and pitmaster, Mike's Bar-B-Q and Sub Shop, Mountain City, Tennessee, from the book **The Place Setting**

For Larry Proffitt, every booth, every door, every corner, and every inch of The Ridgewood bring forth memories. He enters the front door and remembers his late mother and his late brother greeting customers, making change, handing over carryout orders, and turning on the CLOSED sign at nightfall. Memories of his father are perhaps the strongest when Larry walks down to the pit. The structure is well removed from the restaurant building, some 75 yards away.

"People talk about barbecue, and sometimes they talk about cooking it over gas or they talk about cooking it with an electric cooker, but to me, barbecue has the connotation of smoke and fire," says Larry. His words remind me of a line from the book *Southern Food: At Home, On the Road, in History*, written by my friend the late John Egerton, who dined at

Jim Proffitt with his granddaughter Lisa, who now runs the restaurant. Photo courtesy Larry Proffitt.

The Ridgewood when he was doing research for that classic book, first published in 1987. "Barbecue," John wrote, "is as old as fire."

The smoke and fire of hickory wood have always been the essential elements of the Ridgewood enterprise. Hickory is the wood of choice because, as Larry says, "It's a predominant hardwood in these local counties here in East Tennessee. A lot of people mix their wood, but we're simple folks who don't. We believe if something works, don't bother it."

When the Proffitts made the decision to start barbecuing, it was up to Jim to design the pit. He built the first one out of blocks. "Before long, those blocks got saturated with grease, and up in fire it went," Larry recalls. "So the next time he built it, he made it out of bricks. That lasted a while. Then up it went in smoke."

For his final design, Jim chose stainless steel and fire bricks, like the ones used in home fireplaces. Although the pit has been reworked several times over the years, Jim's design from the 1950s is still in use. Fire bricks form the liner, encased in 14 inches of concrete. The top and doors are made of stainless steel. The other elements fall under the category of proprietary secrets.

"The essence of it is, you get a good fire going and shut the air off except for just a miniscule amount, just so that it will lie in there and smolder," Larry explains. "We start a fire early in the morning with kindling and then put on the hickory wood and get the fire to roaring real good. Then we shut the air off and it really starts smoldering. Then we open the pit and put the meat in, on a big, long grate. The key is knowing just how much air to let in, in order to maintain the proper level of heat. There'll be an intense amount of smoke coming out if you

leave it open a few minutes, and if you leave it open too long, you get a big fire, and that's one thing we want to avoid. There's an art to it. It's much more of an art than one would expect. This is not some electric device. It's a real barbecue pit, and you vary the intensity of the heat with the amount of air you let through. It takes a long time and is a lot of work. My mama said it's hard work, and it is."

Hunter Nance and Steve Rains tend Jim Proffitt's original pit design for Ridgewood. Photo by Larry Smith.

Hunter Nance and Steve Rains tend the pits today at The Ridgewood. Both of them grew up within a mile of the restaurant, in opposite directions. Steve says keeping the fire at the right temperature is a "touch and go" enterprise, since it never behaves the same every day. Hunter and Steve say a pitmaster has to deal with and compensate for several variables: the size of the wood, the size of the hams, how many hams are cooking, and how much water is in those hams. It is indeed as much art as it is science.

High on the Hog

"Any country boy knows the difference.
In the country, we turn the shoulders into sausage."
Larry Proffitt

Memphis-style barbecue generally involves the cooking of pork shoulder and ribs. The Ridgewood uses neither. From the beginning, fresh ham has been the porcine cut of choice, despite its higher price. Using shoulder would be contrary to the Proffitt family philosophy. The Proffitts have always used shoulder to make sausage. In the late fall, the Proffitts used to kill four or five hogs, and they provided enough meat—bacon, shoulder, hams, hocks, and ribs—to feed the family all year.

The heading from one of the first Ridgewood menus to feature barbecue proclaimed, "Ridgewood Specializes in the South's Finest Hickory Smoked Pit Cooked Bar-B-Que." In addition to the barbecue meat, the pork dinner included "Golden French Fries, Fresh Homemade Slaw, Ridgewood Bar-B-Que Sauce, Hot Rolls and Butter," all for $1.85. Barbecue beef was 10 cents more. Early menus gave diners the choice of chopped or sliced meat, but the chopped option was later dropped. Larry Proffitt says the slicing imparts more flavor to the meat.

The hams that come in to The Ridgewood for barbecuing today are boned and rolled. Their pre-cooked weight ranges from 10 to 13 pounds each, although for consistent cooking,

The only cut of pork used at The Ridgewood is fresh ham—about 1,000 pounds of it each week, and the servers don't worry about weighing the meat that goes on a Ridgewood barbecue sandwich. Photo by Fred Sauceman.

an attempt is made to buy them as close as possible to the same size.

After about eight hours of cooking, beginning around nine o'clock in the morning, the hams are removed from the pit, allowed to cool a bit, and then they are rubbed with a spice blend and salt. Once the seasoning is complete, the hams are placed in a cooler. The next morning, the meat is sliced with an electric slicer. It is never pulled or chopped or minced. "It's more tender, the way we slice it," says manager Ray Harrington. "With the chopping of a whole hog, like in North Carolina, you don't know what you're getting, whereas ours is all ham. And it's a lot smokier than most meats."

All of the fat is removed from the meat. "There'll be no fat in your barbecue," Larry declares. "The beef's good, but that hog meat's special."

Then comes the sauce.

A Family Heirloom and Rite of Passage: The Sauce

"See, your sauce is your barbecue. People can holler about it but now I just tell you a fact about barbecue, you got to have a sauce. You ain't got a sauce, you ain't got no barbecue. You know, that's where your business is. Them other ingredients, that slaw and that sauce, that makes the barbecue. Now, if you cook barbecue all day long and you ain't got no good sauce, you ain't got no barbecue."

James Willis, who tended the pits for decades, beginning in 1938 when he was fourteen, at Leonard's Barbecue in Memphis, Tennessee. From an oral history by the Southern Foodways Alliance, a unit of the Center for the Study of Southern Culture at the University of Mississippi in Oxford.

**"Just come right on by.
We've got it—pints or quarts or gallons."**

The late Grace Proffitt speaking of sauce, in a feature story aired by WBIR-TV in Knoxville, Tennessee

The Ridgewood barbecue sauce recipe has never been written down, at least not permanently. Its ingredients only exist in the minds of Larry Proffitt and Lisa Proffitt Peters. Imitators

Ridgewood sauce is tomato-based, sweet, sour, and spicy—"good enough to sell," as Larry Proffitt says. Photo by Larry Smith.

abound. "Mock" Ridgewood sauces have been published in books and posted on the Internet. Larry Proffitt has seen those recipes. He appreciates the imitation as the highest form of flattery, but he says none of those recipes is close to the original. One claiming to be a "mock" Ridgewood sauce is about eleven ingredients short of what the original recipe calls for.

The Proffitts describe their storied concoction as "like a Texas sweet-sour-tomatoey-based sauce with a spicy taste to it, but not very hot." The color is reddish-brown.

"It's different from anything you could buy on the market," Larry adds. "I took barbecue to Florida once on a turkey hunt to feed the guys in camp, and I forgot the sauce. I went to the biggest grocery store I could find and bought some of everything I could find, but there wasn't anything close."

Jim Proffitt developed the recipe for Ridgewood sauce, and once he got it perfected, after several stages of tasting, it never changed. It's a long recipe, but the ingredients have always been constant. Grace said it took about six months to perfect the secret recipe.

Retired Criminal Court Judge Arden Hill began eating at The Ridgewood in 1949, the restaurant's second year of operation, after he had graduated from law school. Hill was working for an insurance company at the time, and his business travel often took him through Bullock's Hollow. "It was good then, and it's gotten better ever since," Hill says of The Ridgewood. The judge's fondness for the restaurant has never waned. He still eats there every two or three weeks.

"Larry told me a long time ago—and I've heard him tell it two or three times—that he and his brother were Guinea pigs, and they didn't know it," says Hill. "Their dad would mix two barbecue sauces and call them A and B or 1 and 2 and send one boy to one room and the other to the other room, and Jim would ask each of them, out of the presence of the other, which sauce was better. If they agreed, then they'd discard the other sauce and keep adding until they got the recipe the way they wanted it."

Jim would never commit that recipe to paper. He asked his wife Grace and his sons Larry and Terry to memorize it. "Boy, you might have to use this sauce some time to make a living," Jim often told Larry.

"This is the third generation stirring," says Larry Proffitt of his daughter Lisa. Photo by Fred Sauceman.

In the beginning, the Proffitts made one gallon of sauce at a time. Today, a typical day's batch can run anywhere from thirty to sixty gallons. As Lisa stirs the sauce, her father dips some out in a spoon. The thrill of a new batch has never faded over the years.

"Original recipe. Good enough to sell. Man, that's good. That'll make you lick the spoon. Spicy. That's the way it should be," Larry proclaims.

While an increasing number of barbecue restaurants across the country

Ridgewood's famous sauce—ready to take home. Photo by Fred Sauceman.

offer multiple sauces from different regions, Ridgewood has always served just the one.

As barbecue scholar John Shelton Reed puts it, "Having just one sauce makes sense to me because, number one, it's easier and, number two, it has become a sort of trademark. The Ridgewood isn't Burger King. You can't have it your way. And that's not just the Proffitts. It's true of a lot of the old-time barbecue places. As Sam Jones, owner of the Skylight Inn in Ayden, North Carolina, says, 'It's not what you want, it's how much of it.'"

Ridgewood's barbecued ham has a beautiful whiteness about it. Once it's sliced, the meat is placed on a flat-top grill, the sauce is added, and it's all tossed together. "What ketchup will taste like in heaven" is Reed's description of that sauce.

Each table has a squeeze bottle of sauce, and jars of it sit on top of an old meat counter near the cash register, ready for purchase and use at home. Retired WJCW radio announcer Dave Hogan, who advertised Ridgewood on his morning show for years from the station's studios in Gray, Tennessee, lauds the restaurant's sauce as a dressing for salads. Larry Proffitt says many diners use it instead of ketchup for the restaurant's freshly cut French fries, and customers also report filling their home-baked potatoes with it. The Proffitts hear from people who keep jars of Ridgewood sauce in the refrigerator for late-night snacks, dipping their spoons deep into the jar and eating the product entirely by itself.

The recipe's tomato content, in the form of ketchup, places it squarely in the East Tennessee school of sauce-making. Generally the rule about barbecue sauce geography is this: the farther east you go, into North Carolina, the less tomato the barbecue sauces contain. The Piedmont sauces, or dips, in North Carolina retain some tomato content but certainly not as much as the Ridgewood product. And once you pass The Great Divide and head into Eastern North Carolina, tomatoes virtually disappear, yielding to vinegar and pepper. In East Tennessee, though, tomatoes still rule.

Most sauces native to East Tennessee are strikingly sweet, and many of them achieve that sweetness through the use of sorghum syrup. Tennessee and Kentucky are America's largest producers of the sweet, earthy, floral, amber-colored syrup, made by squeezing the juice from sorghum cane and carefully boiling it down in the fall. The cane's relatively short growing season matches the region's climate perfectly. Sorghum seeds are usually planted in late May, and by September and October, the cane is ready for cutting and squeezing.

Some East Tennessee barbecue sauces are also sweetened with honey. In fact, the local sorghum producer we rely on in Washington County, Tennessee, Arland Johnson, crafts a barbecue sauce that incorporates both sorghum and honey. Clearly, in East Tennessee, sweetness is valued.

I don't possess the Ridgewood sauce recipe and I would never ask for it. Secrets should remain secrets. Its mystery is part of Ridgewood's legacy and lore. I'm content to know that this sauce complements the smokiness of Ridgewood's fresh ham perfectly, and its thickness allows the deep reddish-brown liquid to adhere to the meat with minimal dripping.

For the Proffitts, Ridgewood barbecue sauce is like a family heirloom. One generation teaching it to the next is a rite of passage. A Proffitt has to be old enough, responsible enough, and clearly committed to the future of the business in order to be given the honor and responsibility of learning how to make the sauce.

Terry Proffitt died suddenly, at the age of fifty-five, on June 20, 2002. "He was a big man, and he smoked," Larry says of his brother, who was three years his junior. "He was having passing out spells, but he wouldn't tell a physician. It was atrial fibrillation. Mama had it, too. His heart would stop, and he would pass out and come back to. Well, that happened several times. And he wouldn't address it. And the last time, he just didn't wake up."

The late Terry Proffitt, who memorized the sauce recipe, too. Photo courtesy Larry Proffitt.

Larry remembers his only brother as innovative. With a construction background, he designed a bigger dining room for The Ridgewood and extended the length of the kitchen. "And he was a gentle, happy laugher. People liked him. He was a people person. My father was that way. He was gregarious and outgoing."

To his niece Lisa, Terry embodied the egalitarian spirit of The Ridgewood, even in death. "My husband remarked that he had never seen a funeral where there was such a big gap between the poorest of the poor and the richest of the rich. Terry could relate to anybody."

After Terry's death, the restaurant was closed for ten days that summer of 2002. Closing for that length of time was a rarity. Larry believes it was the longest period of closure in the restaurant's history.

With no one else present in the restaurant, during that period of mourning for his only brother, Larry told his daughter Lisa that it was finally time for him to teach her the sauce recipe. She was thirty-four years old. Two years before, Terry had told his brother it was time to pass the recipe along to Lisa, but Larry responded that it was not time yet.

"So we came over here that afternoon, a Sunday afternoon, and everything was closed, and I wrote the recipe down for her," Larry tells me during my very first interview with him, on June 19, 2003. "She said, 'Do you really remember the recipe?' And I said, 'Do you remember your Social Security number?' I said, 'I've known this recipe since I was sixteen years old. It's been in my head, and now it's going to be in your head.'"

Larry then recited each ingredient and amount, over and over, until Lisa was confident that she knew every item, every step. Together, as she was memorizing that Sunday afternoon, father and daughter made thirty gallons of sauce. Larry then instructed Lisa to write the recipe down on a piece of paper.

"She wrote the recipe down. It's a pretty long recipe. And so she wrote all of it down. Then I went outside and got me a pack of matches. I brought that piece of paper back over to the sink and turned the water on, and I struck a match to the recipe. And I said, 'There goes your recipe. I hope it's in your head. Because it's only in mine and yours now.'

"And so there it resides. Until the next generation."

Lisa required no additional instruction, no reminders to jog her memory. She used a word to remember each item on the list. Even though the recipe involves over twenty different ingredients, it has never left her.

Sammons, a hot dog restaurant in business since 1950 in neighboring Carter County, Tennessee, keeps its chili recipe in a bank vault. Ridgewood's sauce recipe exists only in the minds of two people, until the time comes when Lisa's children reach the right age and the right level of maturity to learn it themselves and the sauce is passed on to what will be the fourth generation of family ownership.

There is no piece of furniture, no plot of land, no item of jewelry, nothing any more precious to the Proffitt family than that sacred sauce. Jim Proffitt was right in his words to his son. There indeed did come a day when that sauce recipe was needed to make a living for the family.

"This is the third generation stirring," Larry proudly announces one morning as we walk back into the kitchen to shoot video for a documentary film about the restaurant. Lisa is making sauce, and that day's output is sixty gallons, which will be gone in less than a week. Just to make sure we fully understand the culinary lineage, Larry repeats, "My daddy came up with that sauce."

A Stellar Endorsement

I first met Ardie Davis in a pasture field. It was in Oxford, Mississippi. In town, really. Only a short walk from the courthouse square. The occasion was the annual Southern Foodways Symposium, held every October on and around the campus of the University of Mississippi and put on by an organization called the Southern Foodways Alliance.

It was 2002, and that year's topic for study and digestion was barbecue. Ardie dispensed wisdom on sauce. That symposium has since come to be referred to as "The Barbecue Summit," attended by no less than Calvin Trillin, whose writing in *The New Yorker* and in his "Tummy Trilogy" of books catapulted Kansas City's Arthur Bryant's Barbeque to worldwide fame. The symposium was a watershed in the world of smoked meats. The "Summit" and its subsequent aftermath of publicity not only helped spur a renewed interest in the art and craft of barbecuing but also contributed to an upsurge in the study of barbecue culture.

Ardie Davis was given the title, that symposium weekend, of Curator of Sauces. It was the perfect choice. Ardie has been named a Barbecue Legend by the renowned *Kansas City Star* newspaper. In 1984, in his backyard, he founded the Diddy-Wa-Diddy National Barbecue Sauce Contest. Eventually that event would be renamed the American Royal International BBQ Sauce, Rub, & Baste Contest. On weekends, Ardie transforms himself into Remus Powers, Ph.B. With his doctorate in barbecue from "Greasehouse University," he judges and oversees competitions nationwide.

As a judge for the Kansas City Barbeque Society, I have repeated Ardie's words often. He is the author of "The Barbecue Oath," which judges repeat, with right hands raised, before every KCBS contest: "I do solemnly swear to objectively and subjectively evaluate each Barbeque meat that is presented to my eyes, my nose, my hands, and my palate. I accept my duty to be an Official KCBS Certified Judge, so that truth, justice, excellence in Barbeque, and the American Way of Life may be strengthened and preserved forever."

Thanks to Ardie Davis, one of America's most knowledgeable barbecue experts, The Ridgewood Restaurant, through its sauce, had a presence during that historic symposium in Mississippi.

In their book *America's Best BBQ: 100 Recipes from America's Best Smokehouses, Pits, Shacks, Rib Joints, Roadhouses, and Restaurants*, Davis and co-author Paul Kirk write, "Our good friend Fred Sauceman has sung the praises of Ridgewood for years. When Ardie was the official Curator of Sauces at the Southern Foodways Alliance symposium on barbecue, Fred readily volunteered to bring a fresh quart of Ridgewood Bar-B-Que Sauce.

"We can still picture Fred holding that jar carefully and reverently. He handed the jar to Ardie like it was a sacred object—which to many Ridgewood fans it is. All but a few drops of Grace Proffitt's famous sauce were consumed that night by enthusiastic symposium participants. We still have the empty jar. The remnants that went begging aren't safe to eat now, but the empty jar with the Ridgewood label is a treasure we cherish.

"Besides our friendship with Fred, we have our own history with the Ridgewood. In 1984, when Ardie founded the Diddy-Wa-Diddy National Barbecue Sauce Contest, he wrote to Grace Proffitt and asked her to enter her sauce in the contest. Grace herself replied, with a nice letter, a newspaper article about the Ridgewood, and a bottle of sauce. We've been Ridgewood fans ever since!"

Davis and Kirk of course don't know the sauce recipe, but they do share my knowledge that it involves over twenty different ingredients. "We chuckle," they write in their book, "when reading the ingredients listed on the label: tomato catsup, salt, sugar, and spices." It's just a start.

A Ridgewood menu from the 1960s, worded with typical mountain humility and understatement, describes Jim Proffitt's creation as "a homemade sauce that's different."

Grace Proffitt got the idea to serve barbecue beans while visiting her son Larry when he was in pharmacy school in Memphis. Photo by Fred Sauceman.

A Prescription for Great Beans

"I hope it goes right on. I have my son here helping me. And I'm almost seventy-three, and of course I work every day. And I enjoy it. I enjoy talking to people. I enjoy having them. And that's my life."

Grace Proffitt, to WCYB-TV, Bristol, Virginia

"You've got to start your meal with a crock of Mrs. Proffitt's barbecue beans."

Dave Hogan, WJCW Radio, Gray, Tennessee

It's been said that you can't make good barbecue and comply with a health code, but Ridgewood defies that maxim. The owners take health codes seriously. Their professional reputations depend on it, in fields far different from cooking barbecue. Ridgewood is a barbecue restaurant run by health care professionals. Larry Proffitt splits his time between stirring sauce at his family restaurant in Bluff City and filling prescriptions at Burgie Drug Store in Elizabethton. His daughter Lisa Proffitt Peters is a registered nurse, and his daughter Rebecca Wilkins is a nurse practitioner. Lisa holds a bachelor's degree and Rebecca a master's, both from East Tennessee State University in nearby Johnson City. Rebecca splits her time between her parents' drug store and an OB/GYN practice in Elizabethton.

Larry says although there are some similarities, like a respect for exactness and attention to detail, his two lines of work are decidedly different.

"It's a rewarding thing when you hear people say you've got really great food," Larry explains. "Whereas to contrast it, in pharmacy, the people you often see are sick. They're sick people. And a lot of them, they become friends over the years. But you see the sick and the sorrowful and the dying. They appreciate the care that you give them, the explanations that you give them, the time you give them when they can't see a doctor. That's rewarding, but for me personally, I grew up in this restaurant. I'd get off the bus right here from school, and I'd come in here and eat supper."

Larry graduated from Mary Hughes High School in the Sullivan County community of Piney Flats. It's a grade school now, having been consolidated into Sullivan East High School. His decision to pursue a career as a pharmacist came after a period of what he calls "rebellion" as a pre-medical student at the University of Tennessee in Knoxville. His life turned when he met his future wife Norma, from LaFollette in Campbell County, Tennessee. After graduating from Draughon's Business College, Norma had gone to work in the office of Kimball's Jewelers in Knoxville. Larry asked his friends Tom and Pat Roush if he could ride with them one night when they were taking Norma home. Larry and Norma started dating thereafter, and what sealed the deal was Grace's blessing. Norma was the only girlfriend to earn Grace's approval. Larry

Barbecue beans, served here by Millie Combs, are a way to use bits of pork left over from the slicing of the meat. Photo by Larry Smith.

and Norma Proffitt celebrated their fiftieth wedding anniversary on June 5, 2016.

Once he got back on the educational track, Larry decided on a career in pharmacy, knowing that after four years of pharmacy school, he could start making an immediate living. He enrolled at the University of Tennessee Center for the Health Sciences in Memphis, then more than a 12-hour drive from his Northeast Tennessee home in the days before the full development of interstate highways. Despite that distance, Grace and Jim visited their son regularly, and Larry would take them out for barbecue, oftentimes at Leonard's, then located on McLemore Avenue in Memphis.

John Egerton called Leonard's "the granddaddy of all the Memphis pits." Leonard Heuberger opened the business in 1922 with five stools, selling barbecue sandwiches for five cents. Leonard's grew quickly, becoming one of the largest drive-in restaurants in the country. Leonard's is generally credited as the creator of the quintessential Memphis barbecue sandwich: pork shoulder meat on a bun with a tomato-based sauce and coleslaw. Elvis Presley was a frequent diner at Leonard's. Current owner Dan Brown says Presley would bring friends for after-hours parties that would last until sunrise. Dan is a true pitmaster, dedicated to his craft and willing to invest the precious time to do it right. He once told me, "If you have to have your beeper (yes, it was a few years ago) attached to your belt or your cellular phone, you have no business going outside to cook barbecue."

During one of their meals at Leonard's in Memphis, the Proffitts ordered barbecue beans. Larry told his mother that she, too, could make good barbecue beans, so she went home and developed the recipe. Her creation has been described as one of the best side dishes in the South.

The making of the beans is another example of Proffitt family frugality. They're flavored with meat scraps and burnt ends. Small pieces of barbecued ham that fall off during the slicing of the meat are mixed into the bean pot, along with Ridgewood's barbecue sauce and a load of onions. Individual servings come in small crocks, as full as they can get. The beans actually serve as a barbecue appetizer, although

Behind the counter at Burgie Drugs in Elizabethton, Tennessee: Rebecca Wilkins and her parents Norma and Larry Proffitt. Photo by Larry Smith.

no one uses that term at The Ridgewood. "One lady I go to church with, she'll get a quart of beans to go, and that's all she'll eat," says Ray Harrington.

"Them beans is the best I've ever eaten," declares racing legend Junior Johnson, as we interview him for our documentary film about The Ridgewood. (Ironically, Junior had a flat tire on the way to the interview.)

Larry Proffitt earned his doctorate in pharmacy from the University of Tennessee Center for the Health Sciences in Memphis in 1969. For three years, he worked for Herman Lubin, a Jewish druggist at Whiteway Pharmacy in Memphis. Although Larry Proffitt and Herman Lubin had a good working relationship, Larry declined Lubin's offer to manage one of his drugstores. Larry had lived through the unrest and violence before, during, and after the assassination of Dr. Martin Luther King, Jr., in Memphis in 1968, and he was ready to come home.

Larry would find his place at Burgie Drug, one of Elizabethton's oldest businesses, opened in 1892 by Harry Burgie. When Burgie died in 1952, Max Jett bought the business. By the time Larry finished pharmacy school, Jett was dying of lung cancer. He and Larry ran the business as partners for a year, and Jett sold it to Larry outright in 1971.

The drug store was originally located in downtown Elizabethton, but Larry says urban renewal destroyed all the parking, so the decision was made to move to the town's outskirts, on G Street. Larry went in with five other people on the venture. He did not have the money to buy all new furnishings and fixtures, so he accommodated the old wooden and glass cabinets and counters from the original drug store. His limited funds turned out to be a blessing. Sections of the drug store of today have the look and feel of a century ago. "I wanted my customers to feel at home," he says. "And they did."

Max Jett made a deep impression on Larry not just as a pharmacist but also as an eater. "Back then, Mama made her own chili for hot dogs," Larry remembers. "Max would order five hot dogs. I can see him right now, all them hot dogs laid side by side on a long platter."

In 1987, when Larry and Terry were reviewing the menu to figure out what should be eliminated, they considered dropping hot dogs. "I asked Mama what she had hot dogs for, and she chewed me out," Larry says. "She said kids eat hot dogs. That makes sense. I had kids then. A kid won't eat just anything, but you lay a hot dog in front of him, even if he's three years old, and he'll eat a hot dog."

When Lisa turned thirteen, her father started giving her chores in the drug store, to get her used to meeting people and talking to them. Down deep, he hoped that experience would prepare her to take over her grandparents' restaurant one day. At the same time, Larry insisted that both his daughters prepare themselves for careers with a high likelihood of employment. After they started college, their father convinced them both to change their majors to nursing. Rebecca would find her permanent career path in health care. At the drug store, she pays the bills like her father has done. Burgie still maintains charge accounts, which Rebecca oversees. Lisa worked as a registered nurse for four years at Northside Hospital in St. Petersburg, Florida, before returning home to learn the restaurant business. Like other employees, she started out bussing tables and washing dishes. "I'm proud of her because she has succeeded, and she has a family, too," Larry says. "She's making it happen every day."

Rebecca will eventually own the drug store. Lisa will eventually own the restaurant. "They're going to pay me for them, and I'll give them half of the money back," Larry notes.

Lisa's children, twins Jacob and Amanda, will follow their mother's path and get to know the pharmacy business, but Jacob has been saying from a young age that he wishes to run The Ridgewood someday.

As Larry finishes a hamburger steak and a half sweet-half unsweet tea in a booth at The Ridgewood, he feels he must explain his lunch choices to me. "I went to the Cleveland Clinic to have my heart worked on, and the cardiologist said, 'Now, you know you're mildly obese.'"

Larry laughs and then the mood turns as he reflects on the life's work of his family, from the perspective of a man who has had too many encounters with death. "We've got enough to live on, and that's all that's important. When they lay us all out, we've got the same thing anyway."

And then that long-developed antipathy to governmental interference emerges again from his mountain soul: "Things change so fast. They're dreaming up new rules for you right now."

I've written stories about pitmasters across the South who have entered the barbecue business from a variety of other professions. One repaired looms. One mined coal. One taught school. One coached football. One sold bait. One sold bread. One even graduated from the Culinary Institute of America. Larry Proffitt and Lisa Proffitt Peters are the only pharmacist-nurse team I know in the business of selling barbecue.

Larry Proffitt as Professor

In the fall of 2016, I took the Foodways of Appalachia course with Fred Sauceman. It fit right into my program of study, and I had been excited to take the course ever since finding out it was offered at East Tennessee State University. A class about food? How can that not be fun? Several weeks into the class, "fun" still remained as one descriptor. Though, if anyone asked me how my experience with Foodways was going, my synapses would probably start firing, and, rather than just saying it was a fun class, I would go on about the connections between food and culture, talking about things like why we eat what we eat, the historical significance of the different kinds of barbecue sauce found across the South, and, oh, guess what? We get to eat in class as well.

The day Larry Proffitt visited our class as a guest lecturer was one of those much-beloved eating days. Off to the side of the room was a row of tables topped with big foil pans stuffed with barbecue pork, barbecue beans, slaw, and blue cheese dressing with crackers to the side. We lined up and filled our paper plates with food before going back to our seats. It was the first time I had eaten anything from Ridgewood Barbecue, as well as the first time I had their distinct, thinly sliced barbecue ham smothered with sweet, tomato-based sauce. The blue cheese dressing was an experience—thick and spoonable with large chunks of cheese. Mr. Proffitt, as guest lecturer, was inspiring. He shared with us the history of Ridgewood and the Proffitt family's passion and dedication to their food, his commitment to quality, and his refusal to cut time by getting pre-packaged barbecue meat.

Once the class came to an end, Mr. Proffitt urged us to take a second (or third) plate home, similar to the way my grandfather does whenever I visit. Mr. Proffitt was a generous man, both in the time he gave our class and in the food portions he offered us. Most of us who pursue a degree like a master of arts in Appalachian Studies have goals of being able to better help our communities. Unfortunately, it's easy to get mired down with researching and writing and suddenly find yourself feeling isolated. Eating barbecue in class and talking about life with restaurant owners

Larry Proffitt talks barbecue with a Foodways of Appalachia class from East Tennessee State University. Photo by Charlie Warden.

was restorative and brought me back home and feeling connected to the community.

—Cathryn Washell, Duluth, Georgia

Thanks to the Appalachian Foodways course, I have a wonderful memory about Ridgewood Barbecue. I am always a little concerned when I try new foods. This is due to my many food allergies. When Larry Proffitt came to the class to speak, he reassured me that an ingredient I was most concerned about was not an ingredient in the sauce. I was so happy that I could try the barbecue that it brought tears to my eyes. I loved the barbecue so much that I got seconds. I did not like blue cheese dressing until that day. I loved the Ridgewood dressing so much, I think I could have drunk it from a cup. Ridgewood Barbecue has now become my favorite restaurant. I not only order a large barbecue sandwich but also the 32-ounce container of blue cheese dressing.

—Joy Gouge, Johnson City, Tennessee

Blue Cheese Bounty

"The atmosphere there is happy and private."
Yujie Liu, Qingdao, China

It doesn't come to the table in a cruet. It doesn't come "on the side" in a small plastic cup. It doesn't come in a squeeze bottle. Blue cheese dressing at The Ridgewood is served in a bowl, lipping full. The sizes are small and large, although large and extra large would be more accurate.

Chinese students from East Tennessee State University begin their Ridgewood meal with blue cheese dressing. Photo by Fred Sauceman.

You don't delicately and slowly pour this blue cheese dressing over a salad. In fact, there is usually no salad. When you order blue cheese dressing at The Ridgewood, the dressing is the focus, not the accoutrement. It's not intended to be poured over anything. Surrounding that bowl of creamy, sharp dressing is a corona of saltine crackers, known to many people in the mountains as "soda crackers." Those crackers are your shovels, your tools. You dunk them deeply into that bowl of blue cheese dressing, getting as much of the product on there as you can.

Among my list of criteria for a good food story is this: a quirky product. Ridgewood's take on blue cheese dressing and that unorthodox serving method qualify.

Ridgewood etiquette dictates dipping saltine crackers into blue cheese dressing. Photo by Fred Sauceman.

"My father had a great push to create something new," says Larry. To Jim Proffitt's list of creations—barbecue sauce and pit design—add blue cheese dressing. Its reputation has grown so over the years that it almost rivals barbecue as a Ridgewood calling card. Before it became an item all its own, it was listed on the menu as Roquefort dressing for "Head Lettuce Salad" and relegated to secondary status in parentheses. Eventually it shed the parentheses and the French name.

"This blue cheese starts out as a big wheel," Larry says. "A seven-pound wheel. When you tear that wrapper off of it and cut into it, it's got a powerful smell. We take a big hoop of blue cheese and cut it into hunks with a butcher knife. And then the kitchen staff will take an old-timey grater and grate that stuff. Boy, that is good," exclaims Larry as he scoops up a cracker full of his father's invention.

Junior Johnson agrees: "Well, the blue cheese dressing, this is the first time I've really had it, and I'll tell you one thing, I could set here and eat that right there with crackers by itself."

It's not unusual for the Ridgewood staff to make six tubs of blue cheese dressing and have to make more the very next day. Lisa says some diners order barbecue sandwiches and large bowls of blue cheese dressing and pour the entire contents of the bowls on top of the sandwiches.

As for the recipe, it's a secret, too. Ridgewood manager Ray Harrington reports that one customer drives all the way from Knoxville, Tennessee, for blue cheese dressing. "And she tried every way in the world to get the recipe," Ray tells me. "And one day she came in and tried to propose to me to get the recipe."

"In all seriousness?" I ask.

"Yes," Ray answers. "I told her I was happily married."

The rejection didn't put an end to her two-and-a-half-hour trips to The Ridgewood.

Placing the Order: A Tale of Two Slaws

"I had a pork barbecue sandwich with fries and coleslaw and blue cheese dip, and it was excellent. I'm glad we came here. We could smell the food from outside already."

Martin Gezdinsky, Prague, The Czech Republic

With its hamburgers and hamburger steaks, catfish, shrimp, baked ham sandwiches, steaks, and more, The Ridgewood has an extensive menu. But I never open it. Ridgewood, to me, means pork barbecue, period. The only question is: sandwich or platter?

The barbecued ham that is troweled between the buns of the sandwich is never weighed. And the price of that sandwich is less than what many of the gas and electricity cooks charge for one lesser in size and heft.

"I'm sure we're not making any money on some of the sandwiches, because those ladies get heavy hands," says Larry with a laugh. "I despise to go in a place and I'm hungry for barbecue or I'm hungry for steak and they give me a little thing I can read a paper through or a little sandwich that's about the size of a lady's hand."

Being attuned to weights and measures as a pharmacist, Larry once tried an experiment. He called in an anonymous

Ridgewood serves two kinds of slaw, a dinner slaw and one for pork and beef barbecue sandwiches. Photo by Fred Sauceman.

Some customers order barbecue sandwiches minus the bun, with slaw on the side. Photo by Jill Sauceman.

order for twelve barbecue sandwiches. He brought his balance scale home from the drug store and removed the meat from each sandwich. He weighed the meat to determine how much of his finished product was going on customers' sandwiches. The smallest amount was nine ounces. The largest amount was eleven ounces.

Unlike most barbecue restaurants, The Ridgewood prepares two different versions of coleslaw, both with fresh heads of cabbage. Bagged, pre-chopped cabbage is never used. The slaw served on the sandwich is thicker, has a higher mayonnaise content, and includes pickle relish. Order a barbecue platter and the prelude is a different kind of slaw, a dinner slaw, which is thinner and is mixed with grated carrots. Platters come piled with French fries, cut fresh and by hand from whole Idaho baking potatoes every morning.

Both slaws, with their mayonnaise content, are representative of the East Tennessee region and are typical of what would be found at church suppers and family covered-dish dinners. Again, following John Shelton Reed's rule that barbecue in the South changes every 100 miles or so, the mayonnaise tends to disappear as you head into the North Carolina Piedmont, where slaws are often flavored with vinegar, ketchup, and hot sauce.

For years, the master Ridgewood barbecue sandwich builder was Marie Moore. At one point, four members of her family worked at the restaurant. When advanced age prevented Marie from standing on her feet for long periods of time, the Proffitts did not send her home. Instead, she was given a job rolling silverware in napkins, a necessary and daily task at the restaurant. Larry would pass her sandwich-making knowledge on to his other employees.

"I gathered all my cooks together and said, 'I don't care if I don't sell a dozen barbecues a week, we're going to all start cold. It's going to come a la carte, and we're going to fix it just like Marie.' Everybody said Marie had the best sandwiches. There's an art to making the right barbecues. There's a delicate balance to make the right product."

Ray Harrington, the man up front. Photo by Larry Smith.

An average customer count at The Ridgewood for a day is about 500. Ray Harrington, the man up front at the cash register nowadays, sees most all of them. Ray has literally performed every job in the restaurant. Like Lisa Proffitt Peters herself, he started out bussing tables. He has washed dishes. He has sliced

"These fries that you'll eat tonight, they started out as potatoes this morning." —Larry Proffitt. Photo by Fred Sauceman.

potatoes and made fries. He has made beans. He has sliced meat. And he has even tended the pit. Ray and his family have a long history with The Ridgewood. His grandmother, Phyllis Plank, owns the property directly across the road. His grandfather, Bud Plank, would drive his tractor to the restaurant to get sandwiches in the 1950s.

When they were farming and working in the hayfields, Ray and his family would order takeout. They rarely took time to sit down in the restaurant and eat. Ray remembers coming into The Ridgewood with his parents, Joe and Linda Harrington, to pick up those to-go orders. "Terry would be on the register. Customers would often be parked in our driveway, which is down here across from the pits. Dad would get his wallet out to pay for the food, and as Terry would hand the food to him, he'd say, 'Here's your rent.' He'd give us those to-go orders to pay us back for people using that driveway."

Ray spends as much time as anyone in the restaurant now, but he still prefers the taste of a carryout sandwich. "My favorite thing is the pork sandwich. A few people have nicknamed it 'The Ray Special.' I have them put extra slaw on it and extra sauce, so it's juicy and it's running down your elbow. I like mine wrapped to go because everything mingles together and soaks in. That's the way I was raised with them. And even the French fries, I have to have them wrapped up so they'll get a little soggy, and then I eat them with the blue cheese dressing."

Using the dressing as a ketchup substitute is catching on. Former WCYB-TV reporter and anchor Olivia Caridi, who is now pursuing a modeling career in New York City, describes herself as a French fry connoisseur. "When I first moved to Bristol, I was walking around State Street and asked several people where I should eat. They all mentioned Ridgewood. The French fries were amazing. On my second visit, I was told I had to try the blue cheese dressing, and I put it on everything. I was there a lot. I was willing to wait in line sometimes forty minutes to an hour just to eat there."

Ray Harrington says for dine-in, about 70 percent of customers order pork and 30 percent beef. For to go, he says the percentage of pork spikes up to about 90.

"It's astronomical the number of to-go orders that we do," says Ray, who doubles as the Vice Mayor of Bluff City. "For most of those orders, I know what they want when I hear the voice. They'll call on the phone and I've already written down what they want and their name before they can even tell me."

It's not unusual for customers to drive three hours for a load of meat and sauce to take home.

Raised on Ridgewood

I was raised on Ridgewood as a youngster growing up in Carter County. Back then, we had to negotiate the old Bullock's Hollow Highway from Elizabethton to get a taste of Ridgewood. But snaking our way around the curves of that two-lane blacktop was well worth it when we found the barbecue pot of gold at the end of that wooded rainbow.

I never outgrew Ridgewood. Never came close. Never wanted to. Who would? And when I grew up and had three children of my own, I was sure to expose them to two important things: Ridgewood Barbecue and rock and roll music 1970s style, two very vital staples.

During the summers while I was a feature reporter at the local CBS television affiliate, WJHL, each of my kids had his or her turn going along with me on story shoots. In the midst of many of those cherished summer days, it was quite often that we'd eat lunch at Ridgewood.

When my son Trevor was in college, he would often take a much-needed break from his studying and we'd venture over to Ridgewood. Many great conversations were mixed with the barbecue and beans as we solved, or at least attempted to solve, some of the world's problems. We always ordered the same thing from the Ridgewood menu: three pork sandwiches (we'd split the third one and take it home with us) and a big order of fries. My son grew to love Ridgewood almost as much as I do. But my daughters, Andrea and Adrianne, aren't too far behind in their affection for that hickory-smoked goodness.

Yes, I'll admit it. I've had a lifelong love affair with Ridgewood Barbecue. Since that first taste, I'll never get over it. And now the tasty tradition is heading toward coming full circle. These days, I get to talk about Ridgewood every weekday morning on a local radio talk show that I co-host on 910 AM WJCW. Larry Proffitt is a treasured friend who made the decision to advertise his historic restaurant as one of our main sponsors. Talking about Ridgewood is almost as good as eating it. Almost. As I like to say when I talk about Ridgewood on the radio, it's the best barbecue you'll ever slap a lip over!

—Tim Cable, WJCW Radio, Gray, Tennessee

Ridgewood and Racing

"It's Thursday. Junior will be by today."

The late Grace Proffitt,
speaking of NASCAR Hall of Famer Junior Johnson

The Ridgewood Restaurant is located less than fifteen minutes from the Bristol Motor Speedway, known as "the world's fastest half mile." It is the fourth largest sports venue in America and the eighth largest in the world. Some 160,000 people can watch a race at the speedway, known for its steep banking. The first NASCAR race at what is now BMS took place on July 30, 1961.

NASCAR and barbecue somehow naturally go together. Both are clearly and proudly rooted in the American working class. During race weeks in April and August at Bristol Motor Speedway, The Ridgewood is at its fullest.

"The racetrack has been very good for us," Larry asserts. "Over the years, many, many drivers and fans have come here to eat. They went from here to North Carolina, and this was on the way to Charlotte. In the last twenty years, NASCAR has really taken off. If Dale Earnhardt, Jr., comes in, you'll have a mob here. You might as well shut down for the night.

Ridgewood is located less than fifteen minutes from Bristol Motor Speedway. Photo by Angela Jones, Johnson City Press. *Used with permission.*

"We have people come in from Ohio, Florida, within a twelve-hour drive time. A lot of people from Pennsylvania come. They like racing a lot in Pennsylvania. Race fans and drivers have been a big help to us, and we appreciate it."

Pointing to one of the front booths in the restaurant, Larry says, "I've seen Darrell Waltrip sitting right up here. And Junior Johnson would come here. He would stop in regularly with his wife Flossie on Thursdays."

During our video shoot, on March 17, 2011, Junior confirms that he was the first person to bring Darrell Waltrip to The Ridgewood. "Him and his wife came back a lot of times," Junior tells me. "They'd come here before they'd go to the racetrack."

Junior admits that Bullock's Hollow was once a convenient and secluded spot for running illegal whiskey. "Right up on the hill here, I have unloaded whiskey many times. Yeah. That's right. Yes, sir. Heck fire, that was back in the early 1940s."

In 1956, Johnson was convicted of manufacturing non-tax-paid whiskey after being arrested at his father's still in North Carolina. He

Ridgewood was a regular stop for NASCAR legend Junior Johnson (right), shown here with Larry Proffitt. Photo by Larry Smith.

was never caught while running bootleg whiskey on the roads. He said his arrest occurred when his father sent him to the family still to light the fire. Johnson served eleven months in the federal penitentiary in Chillicothe, Ohio, before his release in October 1957. In 1986, Johnson was given a presidential pardon by President Ronald Reagan.

As we were video-recording Junior for our documentary *Smoke in the Holler: The Saucy Story of Ridgewood Barbecue*, he came out with a revelation. Given the passion and the regional chauvinism that exist over barbecue in his home state of North Carolina, I immediately checked the video equipment to make double sure we had captured Junior's revelatory utterance, and we had: "You can go anywhere you want to and get barbecue. I don't think it'd beat this."

The endorsement was simple and sincere. And for a Tennessean like me, it was certainly uplifting. It's a line I've quoted often in talks about barbecue culture around the region. At the same time, I point out that Ridgewood is the only out-of-state barbecue place mentioned by Tennesseans John Shelton Reed and Dale Volberg Reed in their 2008 book *Holy Smoke: The Big Book of North Carolina Barbecue*.

Thursday was typically Junior Johnson's day to stop for Ridgewood barbecue when he was anywhere near the area. He would eat a full meal in the restaurant and then take a bag home with him.

Another favorite NASCAR driver of the Proffitt family was the late Benny Parsons, from Wilkes County, North Carolina, the same county where Junior Johnson grew up. Ridgewood was one of the first restaurants Parsons covered for his "Buffet Benny" segments on ESPN.

"When I come to Bristol," he told viewers, "not only am I looking forward to two great races on Saturday and Sunday, but I can't wait for Friday and lunch at The Ridgewood Restaurant. Great barbecue.

Now everyone all over the world says they've got the best barbecue. How do you tell? I don't know except look for the cooker beside the restaurant. That means they do their own thing, and they've got their own recipe, and most of it is pretty doggone good. Well, Grace Proffitt has been cooking barbecue here for forty-three years.

"Thank you very much, Grace," Parsons says as she brings forth a platter of food into the camera shot. "Look at this—barbecue pork, barbecue beef. The French fries are homemade, great homemade coleslaw, homemade beans."

Larry Proffitt laughed when Benny Parsons told him later that Grace was totally unfamiliar with ESPN and charged him and all the members of the crew for their meals. Larry wrote Benny a letter afterward offering to feed him and the crew on the house any time they dropped by.

For the program book sold at the night race in Bristol one August, Parsons wrote an entire column about Ridgewood:

> It's another hot August night at the Thunder Valley campground, and you've got a great view of the Bristol Motor Speedway facility from your campsite. There's only two more days until THE RACE.
>
> You're standing by the grill, tongs in hand, and those smoking chicken breasts are looking mighty black. The wife, arms crossed, sitting a few feet away in her lounge chair, is eyeballing you in a most threatening manner. It just might be that she's had her fill of "burnt" for this race week. It's time to take some serious action! Heck, forget about saving the marriage, we're talking about saving your life. Dump some water on that fire, and hit the road for some real food.
>
> Just a hop, skip and jump from the track is the greatest little barbecue restaurant in the world. Ridgewood's the name, barbecue is the game. Over exaggerating when I say "greatest little barbecue restaurant in the world"? How many restaurants do you know that have been written up in the pages of *Food and Wine*, *Southern Living* and *People* magazines and in *USA Today*, the "nation's newspaper"?

> Ridgewood is a full service restaurant offering steak, chicken, pork chop, shrimp, oyster and catfish dinners. . . . But it's the barbecue that everyone comes to eat. . . .
>
> I'm not sure whether Ridgewood serves desserts because I've never been in position to want one. . . . If, however, you are inclined to want dessert after partaking, just eat a little more coleslaw. It's just like candy.
>
> As you probably know, food presentation is a very important aspect of all fine cooking. All your great chefs are into it when it comes to giving the meal an attractive look. You know what I mean. "Presentation" is that curly cued little carrot (which you're not supposed to eat), about the size of a spark plug, that's sitting next to those two quarter-sized meat "medallions" and three slices of squash that makes up your $45 entrée at Jacques of New York.
>
> Well, I'm here to tell you that the "chefs" at Ridgewood have got "presentation" down pat. That big ol' hangin' barbecue sandwich, about as big around as a Frisbee and loaded with slaw, is sitting smack dab in the middle of your plate just waiting for you to gobble it up. Add some of those beans, fries on the side, and wash it down with Mrs. Proffitt's terrific iced tea, and we're forgetting all about that little problem you were having with your version of "blackened" chicken just an hour ago.
>
> The atmosphere is comfortable casual, the décor Formica and vinyl.

NASCAR driver Benny Parsons is memorialized in a signed photograph behind the cash register at The Ridgewood. Photo by Fred Sauceman.

After Grace Proffitt's health forced her to leave her business for an assisted-living facility in Elizabethton, when race week came around, she continued to ask about Benny Parsons. As Larry says, "He never forgot his roots. I like people who haven't forgotten their roots."

Benny Parsons died in Charlotte, North Carolina, on January 16, 2007, at the age of sixty-five. His photograph occupies a permanent spot on the wall at The Ridgewood.

Long before he became Vice President for Public Affairs at Bristol Motor Speedway, Clintwood, Virginia, native Kevin Triplett was a fan of Ridgewood Barbecue. In April 2015, he became Commissioner of the Department of Tourist Development for the State of Tennessee.

"The Ridgewood has been a part of my diet for more than thirty years," Commissioner Triplett writes. "We have eaten there to celebrate significant family milestones, and Ridgewood barbecue has graced our table at more holiday and church gatherings than we can count. If I ever pass out, don't worry with ammonia. Just uncap a pint jar of Ridgewood sauce and wave it under my nose. I will be fine.

"Visitors making that trek up the holler in Bluff City know they are close before they ever see the building. They know it by the smell. Guests from all over the country and world continue to make the turn up that holler to smell the smell and taste the food. And for that, we are mighty glad."

Grace on the Job

"The thing that I've learned the most is to stay with what's proven. It's just good food and no mystery."
Larry Proffitt

Grace Proffitt provided much-needed employment for people up and down the hollow and beyond, even if they didn't have a way to get to work. More than once, the restaurant has employed three generations from the same family.

After she graduated from Elizabethton High School in 1970, Brenda Fagan set out to find a job. She had a cousin who worked at The Ridgewood, as well as an aunt. Brenda's aunt stopped by her house and told her if she wanted a job, to go get her uniform and shoes and come in on Saturday morning. Brenda had never met Grace Proffitt, but she was hired on the spot. She has never left, after well over four decades.

Brenda doesn't wait tables any longer. Bad knees and ankles prevent

Grace Proffitt converted The Ridgewood from roadhouse to barbecue restaurant. Photo courtesy Larry Proffitt.

Grace Proffitt provided transportation to and from work for her employees in the early years. As this picture from 1959 shows, having air-conditioning was a big selling point for restaurants during that era. Shown here are, left to right, an unidentified employee, Bertha Dempsey, and Helen Glover. Bertha was the great-aunt of Hunter Nance, one of Ridgewood's current pitmasters. Photo courtesy Larry Proffitt.

that. But true to form, the Proffitts have carved out a special place for her, and she now holds the title of manager, overseeing staff and interacting with customers, since so many of them have become her friends over the years. Occasionally she will use her body to shield a racecar driver from fans with smart phone cameras until the driver can finish his barbecue.

"The first year I worked, I didn't have a car," says Brenda. "Grace picked me up in the mornings and again in the afternoons until I saved up the money for a down payment and bought my first brand-new car, a Ford Pinto."

The Proffitts lived in a brick house on the hill behind the restaurant, close enough for Grace herself to walk to work when she wasn't providing a rural taxi service. Larry still owns the house and property. Wood for the barbecue pits is stored under a shed near the house.

"In the 1950s, many families didn't have a car," Larry remembers. "Here we are, a restaurant out in the country, and we had one car. Well, Mama bought another car, a 1952 Ford station wagon, because there was a lot of people around here, ladies who were at home who would like to work. And we needed help. So she would hire them, and then she would go pick them up. In the morning she'd leave early to make the rounds, picking up usually four or five employees. Then at night she had to take them home. She might not get home until eleven o'clock at night. Those were long days."

Ridgewood has always been a matriarchal barbecue place. It was Grace's restaurant, and she set the rules. John Shelton Reed relates the story of a group of men from Eastman Chemical Company in Kingsport, Tennessee, who drove over to The Ridgewood for lunch. "They were seated," he reports, "but for some reason, they switched tables. Time passed and no one took their order. Mrs. Proffitt was standing there with her arms folded. Finally, one of the men told her they had to get back to work and asked when they could expect to order. She said, 'I'll take your order when you sit where I put you.'"

Jim Hall III, who rides his motorcycle from his home in Mauldin, South Carolina, for lunch at Ridgewood every Saturday, tells of the time when car dealer Joe Sheffield was paying his bill at the restaurant and Grace's security alarm at her house went off. Joe offered to go up the hill and check it out. Jim says Grace reached under the counter, got her pistol, and told Joe, "Here, take this." Joe returned soon thereafter, reporting that a vacuum-cleaner salesman had knocked on the door and triggered the alarm.

Although many customers and former employees recall Grace unceremoniously locking the restaurant's doors at closing time no matter how many people were still waiting in line to eat, many more reflect on her generosity and kindness.

"My mama would let people borrow a little money until payday," says Larry. "My brother would. My daughter does. Employees will get tight on funds and want to borrow twenty-five dollars, fifty dollars until payday."

Grace's management philosophy was simple. She always made it clear that employees worked with her, not for her. "She was

Grace Proffitt, in her familiar uniform, at her sacred space, behind the cash register. Photo courtesy Larry Proffitt.

Brenda Fagan (left) reflects on her long Ridgewood career with Lisa Peters and Larry Proffitt. Photo by Larry Smith.

always good to me," Brenda says as she looks back on the days when she would sit up front with Grace at the cash register.

That helping-one-another philosophy is a Proffitt family trait. When Brenda's son Eric was sick as a child, Larry would make trips to Burgie Drugs at two and three o'clock in the morning to get his medicine.

In turn, as Grace aged, Brenda would drive the lead car to the Proffitt home, with Grace following closely behind. Brenda made sure Grace got safely into the house. And then the routine began again the next morning.

When Brenda had to be off from work for six weeks in 1990, the Proffitts saved a place for her on the restaurant's staff. Because of weight gain after surgery, Brenda was forced to buy new clothes. Terry brought money to help her out. "He was one of the kindest, sweetest men I ever knew," she reflects.

Brenda points out that her story is representative of countless employees over the years whose lives have been made better by the Proffitt philosophy and way of doing business. Larry adds, "It doesn't cost anything to be good to people. It doesn't cost anything to say, 'I appreciate you.'"

Grace's compassion, though, didn't keep her from being what Larry calls "a serious-minded" businesswoman. She ran the business with a tight hand. Operating in a rural area where incomes were generally not high, she was careful to buy only what she needed and to avoid loading the menu with items that would not sell. Take dessert, for example. Still today, there is no cake. There is no pie. There is no ice cream. "People's too full," Grace said. Desserts are limited to the mints and candies available at the register. Says manager Ray Harrington, "People who've never been here before ask about dessert, and I say, 'Just wait until after you eat and ask me again.'"

Steeped in Great Depression frugality, Grace was a saver, and she was full of Southern Appalachian tenacity. In 1987, the two-lane road where the restaurant is located, connecting Elizabethton to Bluff City, was bypassed. A new four-lane highway was constructed about a mile and a half away from the restaurant. Many people predicted that the new road would mean the end of The Ridgewood. Some told Grace she would go broke. Grace refused to give in to those predictions of doom, even though the business lost about $30,000 that year. Ridgewood would make it, she said, since she was not in debt to anyone. "Just wait until they get that road open," she would say, with defiant optimism.

She was right. When the new road opened, her business boomed, even with no Ridgewood sign on the highway. The road suddenly gave diners much easier access to the restaurant. Grace's wisdom and patience had paid off again.

Some national exposure had also helped. For in the July 18, 1983, issue of *People* magazine, between stories about First Lady Nancy Reagan's real father and James Bond's Babes, there appears a piece by Jane and Michael Stern about American regional food. Grace Proffitt is pictured in front of The Ridgewood, holding a platter laden with barbecue beans, slaw, fries, and a pork barbecue sandwich. The story is structured in question-and-answer format. One of the questions is, "Where did you find the best barbecue?" Michael responds, "The best barbecue is at the Ridgewood Restaurant in Bluff City, Tenn.

Dianna Blumenstock came to work at The Ridgewood shortly after the death of Grace Proffitt. She says her customers become like family. Photo by Larry Smith.

It's a pig epiphany. The pork shoulder is cooked in a haze of smoldering hickory wood and is served with sparkling cole slaw and hand-cut French fries."

Although Stern was eating barbecued fresh ham and not pork shoulder, the publicity attracted diners from all over the country and beyond and resulted in a telephone call that would cause Grace to take a rare trip out of Bullock's Hollow. The call was from *Good Morning America*.

"They want me to be on and cook for Joan Lunden," Grace reported to Larry.

"So they flew us to New York City and put us up on Times Square in some kind of big old hotel," Larry recalls.

As Grace said in an interview for WCYB-TV, the NBC affiliate in Bristol, Virginia, "They invited me to come to New York to be on *Good Morning America*. So we went up there, my son and I, and we looked like a couple of gypsies when we got on the plane. They kept calling from New York saying bring this and bring that, and we had all kinds, we had beef and pork. We had barbecue sauce and beans and slaw and everything. That's what they wanted, a little of everything. So we took it and had a big time."

Describing the creation of her family's sauce to *Good Morning America* host Joan Lunden, Grace said, "It wasn't just right at first. We just kept adding this and adding that until we got it just right."

"Let me see if they got it just right," Lunden responded as she forked up some of the meat and sauce. "This is one of the advantages of doing this show. This smells so good....You know something, that's good."

"At its best," Stern told Lunden, "American food is really sleeves-up eating."

Grace Proffitt's grave marker. Photo by Fred Sauceman.

Accustomed to feeding folks whose days were dominated by hard manual labor, Grace Proffitt had learned that lesson long before her New York City television appearance.

Although the telephone would not stop ringing after her return to Northeast Tennessee, Grace remained unfazed and unchanged by the Big Apple experience. Throughout her career, she took brushes with celebrities in stride. Photographer Jeff Sturgill had finished a shoot at Sycamore Shoals Hospital in Elizabethton and stopped at The Ridgewood for a meal. He looked out the window and saw "a beautiful shining new silver bus with a huge blue star on the side." The Dallas Cowboys had come for barbecue. Jeff offered to retrieve his Hasselblad camera from the car and take a picture of Grace with the team, free of charge. "Naw, I don't want no old picture," she told him. Although Jeff was crushed, the disappointment did not end his Ridgewood visits.

In the late 1990s, Larry Proffitt began to notice a decline in his mother's health. Atrial fibrillation, a family trait, had taken hold of her heart. And she began having a series of TIAs—transient ischemic attacks. "She had one at the restaurant," Larry recalls. "She blinked several times and then started looking around like she had come out of a dream. She started talking soon after, but she was never a deep thinker after that. Then they got more severe."

Grace went from the restaurant to the hospital and then to a nursing home. She would never return to her beloved restaurant. Senile dementia had set in. When the atrial fibrillation worsened, Larry says medical personnel wanted to stop his mother's heart and paddle her back, but he would not let them. "I said, 'She'll either convert on the drugs she's been taking, or we'll bury her.'"

Grace Reynolds Proffitt died on Saturday, March 29, 2003, at Sycamore Shoals Hospital in Elizabethton, Tennessee. She was eighty-five years old. She is buried in Monte Vista Burial Park in Johnson City, Tennessee.

Reflecting on the lessons Grace taught her, Lisa says the best way she can pay tribute to her grandmother is to keep the restaurant and its menu just like they are. "I want to make everything as consistent as it was when my grandmother was alive and Terry was alive."

Server Dianna Blumenstock came to work at The Ridgewood just a few days after Grace Proffitt's death. She says the spirit of the enterprising barbecue matriarch is ever present at the restaurant. "We have customers who come weekly, monthly, or more," she says. "Some just come during race week or on a visit to Speedway in Lights [a fundraiser for Children's Charities and one of the largest light shows in the South] up at the track. Some we know on a first-name basis. Those who come weekly usually have the same thing every time. Most people come for the barbecue and some just for the beans or blue cheese. Sometimes they will bring us all a cake to share, or, at Christmas, homemade candy and cookies. Some special customers have brought us plants, jewelry, and cards.

"We have the best customers. When we think of someone we have not seen in a while, we wonder about them. They become like family to us."

The Ridgewood Rundown

"Ambiance only goes so far when your belly is growling."

Larry Proffitt, as told to oral historian Amy Evans with the Southern Foodways Alliance, February 23, 2009

Note that the name is Ridgewood, with no "s" on the end. And it isn't Woodridge, which is the name of a mental health facility in Johnson City. Dianna Blumenstock says that back when the restaurant took personal checks, a customer once made his out to Woodridge. "It made everyone standing around laugh."

Ridgewood founding date: 1948
Founders: Grace and Jim Proffitt
Current owners: Lisa Proffitt Peters and Larry Proffitt
Number of employees: More than 30
Address: 900 Elizabethton Highway, Bluff City, Tennessee 37618
Telephone number: 423-538-7543
Operating hours:
Sunday: CLOSED. In the words of Larry Proffitt, "It's the Lord's day."
Monday through Thursday: 11:00 a.m. to 7:30 p.m.

Friday: 11:00 a.m. to 2:30 p.m., 4:30 p.m. to 8:30 p.m.
Saturday: 11:00 a.m. to 2:30 p.m., 4:30 p.m. to 8:30 p.m.

Ridgewood is typically closed for vacation the first full week of June and is closed during most major holidays. Call the number above for specific questions about operating hours.

Larry Proffitt says, "When I go out, I want good food and plenty of it." At his own restaurant, he practices what he preaches. Photo by Fred Sauceman.

Getting There

"You know you're getting close when you smell the hickory smoke down in the holler."

Dave Hogan, WJCW Radio

In Appalachia, we have a practice of taking one route to get to a destination and a completely different one upon returning—not to confuse or disorient traveling companions but rather to show off the beauty of the region.

There are several ways to get to The Ridgewood, all with their own stunning scenery. My favorite, coming from Johnson City, is to take Highway 400, Unaka Avenue. It's one of the most beautiful drives in the region and stretches through an area deep in history. On the right, in the community of Watauga,

My favorite route to The Ridgewood is Highway 400 through the community of Watauga, where you'll pass St. John Milling Company, once Tennessee's oldest business. Photo by Larry Smith.

Another Highway 400 landmark is the Brick Christian Church. Its name reflects East Tennessee "call it what it is" straightforwardness. Photo by Larry Smith.

is St. John Milling Company, once the oldest continuously operating business in the state of Tennessee. It remained in business for over 230 years. Across the road is the stone house of Jeremiah Dungan, who came down from Bucks County, Pennsylvania, in the 1770s and built the mill on Brush Creek. The mill survived the bullets of Carter's Raid during the Civil War. Ron Dawson, owner of the mill, believes it was spared during that battle on New Year's Eve in 1862 because it functioned then as a church, with services led by a Dunkard minister. Not far from the mill, historians believe, was the site where the first independent government in America, the Watauga Association, was founded.

Taking this route, you'll pass through the hamlet of Turkeytown, and you'll notice a testament to East Tennessee directness: a brick church called The Brick Christian Church. Where Highway 400 intersects the old Elizabethton Highway in a perfect T, turn left. You will cross Indian Creek twice and eventually head from Carter County into Sullivan County. The Ridgewood is on the left.

From Broad Street in Elizabethton, a turn onto North Lynn Avenue, away from town, affords a direct shot to The Ridgewood.

Another option from the Johnson City area is to take Highway 381N (State of Franklin Road), then merge onto 19W/11E toward Bristol. Go through the community of Piney Flats and then turn right onto 19E-South toward Elizabethton. Go about 1.3 miles and turn right onto the old Elizabethton Highway, a two-lane. Nowadays, there is a small green and white sign pointing in the direction of the restaurant. The Ridgewood will be on the right, approximately a quarter mile.

Coming from North Carolina, stay on 19E-North. About seven miles past the intersection with Highway 67, turn left onto the old Elizabethton Highway.

An American Story

I first interviewed Larry Proffitt on June 19, 2003, less than three months after the death of his mother Grace. We sat on the sidewalk outside the restaurant that beautiful late spring morning, watching the sun warm the hollow and witnessing the daily ritual of renewal that every restaurant owner knows. Since then, I have been in Larry's presence often, and, as I am quick to tell him, each time we are together, I learn something new. But I also come away from our encounters with an ever-deepening appreciation for values that are very old. Frugality, fairness, devotion to God and the church, love of family, respect for those who work for a living—these ancient Appalachian traits have drawn me to Bullock's Hollow even more powerfully than the promise of a plate of barbecue.

If this book reads like a love letter to a place and to a family and to the products of their ingenuity, I offer no apology. That was my intent. Being chosen to write this book, to be the person through

Above, my first interview with Larry Proffitt, June 19, 2003. Below, fresh ham and secret sauce on the griddle. Photos by Larry Smith.

Grace Proffitt, seated at right, not long after she started her pioneering business in Bullock's Hollow. Photo courtesy Larry Proffitt.

whom this family's legacy is shared, is one of my life's greatest honors. I am drawn to that stunningly gorgeous hollow by the allure of smoky pork. I am equally called there by the need for connection—to the past and to my mountain culture. Through this food, I am even connected to people I have never known. Visiting Ridgewood today, I understand Grace Proffitt's stubborn refusal to let threats of new roads and the encroachment of quick cooking techniques in America change her business, even though she never personally served me a meal. I think about the risks the Proffitts took over the years and the overriding motivation to keep the business going—as Grace put it, to raise those two little boys. I consider the creativity of barbecue sauce, blue cheese, and proprietary pits, all devised and nurtured in between shifts at a rayon plant.

It is an Appalachian story. It is an American story.

Acknowledgments

This book is as much about family as it is about food. My respect and admiration for the Proffitt family grew as this book grew, as layers of their Appalachian story unfolded. Larry Proffitt is the soul, the spirit, and the intellect behind this project. Of the hundreds of interviews I have done over the years as a journalist, my sessions with him stand out. Since 2003, I have interviewed him on well over a dozen occasions. He has given me hours and hours of his time, answering every question with absolute honesty and accuracy. His memory for details, of events that happened more than half a century ago, is clear. His wisdom is wide-ranging, from pharmaceutical science to farming. His knowledge is encyclopedic, from NASCAR to turkey hunting.

My only regret is that I started this book long after Larry's parents, Grace and Jim Proffitt, had died. But during all those interviews, Larry made them come alive to me. I feel like I have known them. This book is my own small way of making sure that the Ridgewood customers of today understand and appreciate who they were and why they succeeded. The Proffitts have always been a family defined by the dignity of hard work. I cherish their legacy.

I wish to thank Lisa Proffitt Peters for allowing us to visit her family's restaurant many times with cameras, recorders, and notepads in hand, while the business of the day, feeding folks, went on around us. I am glad she chose to carry on her grandmother's life's work.

Ray Harrington is not blood kin to the Proffitts, but you would never know it. As he presides over transactions at the cash register up front, he occupies a cherished spot, where Grace once stood. I am grateful for his hospitality and for his love of The Ridgewood, so obvious in everything he does to help make the restaurant work.

Brenda Fagan seems like a part of the Proffitt family, too, having taken her first job under the tutelage of Grace back in 1970. I appreciate Dianna Blumenstock's smiling service and good stories. To them and to all current and former employees, I thank you.

Larry Smith, a loyal Ridgewood customer in his own right, generously provided many of the photographs that are included in this book. Larry and I have traveled hundreds of miles over the years, documenting the foodways of Appalachia. Along with colleague Charlie Warden, we produced a documentary film about The Ridgewood, which led to the idea of publishing a book-length history of the restaurant.

Long before they ever tasted a platter of smoky, saucy Ridgewood ham, the staff members at Mercer University Press embraced this project and encouraged it along. This is our fifth book together, in a rewarding relationship that extends back now over a decade. Mercer University Press has given voice to so many people in Appalachia through these books. I am eternally grateful to Dr. Marc Jolley, Marsha Luttrell, Jenny Toole, Mary Beth Kosowski, Candice Morris, Burt & Burt Studio, and all the many fine people who make Mercer University Press an American gem.

My wife Jill Sauceman has been a full partner in this book project—asking questions during interviews, taking photographs, offering ideas and insights, and helping to make this journey such a great joy. As I finish this book, we look forward to telling her story of perseverance in a future one.

As my friend George Black once told me, "Knowing the history behind it makes the food taste even better." I am grateful to all the people who have helped me make that connection.

—Johnson City, Tennessee, July 2016

THE ORIGINA
Ridgewood
BARBECUE
OPEN